chocolate

igloo

igloo

Published by Igloo Books Ltd
Cottage Farm
Sywell
NN6 0BJ
www.igloo-books.com

10 9 8 7 6 5 4 3 2

ISBN: 978 1 84817 637 9

Project Managed by R&R Publications Marketing Pty Ltd

Food Photography: R&R Photostudio (www.rrphotostudio.com.au)
Recipe Development: R&R Test Kitchen

Front cover photograph © Stockfood/J. Rynio

Printed and manufactured in India

contents

introduction

Chocolate and cocoa are made from cocoa beans, the seeds of the tropical cacao tree. This tree originates from Central America, and is known scientifically as Theobroma cacao. Theobroma, meaning literally 'food of the gods', is a highly appropriate name for the cocoa bean, the source of such delicious cakes, biscuits and drinks and other sweets.

Since Aztec times people have enjoyed the distinctive flavours produced from the cocoa bean, and its discovery has to rate as one of the most influential food discoveries of all time. Bahia, in eastern Brazil, and the Ivory Coast of Africa currently produce almost half of the world's cocoa beans.

Advances in processing over the years have resulted in the availability of a huge variety of wonderful products, from exquisite Swiss chocolates to warming cocoa drinks and quick pick-me-up chocolate bars.

During the production process, cocoa pods are harvested and then broken open, releasing the seeds. The seeds are fermented for two to ten days to develop flavour, and then dried, graded, packed and shipped to all corners of the world.

Chocolate manufacturers select seeds from various areas to obtain consistent style and flavour. The selected seeds are cleaned and blended, then roasted to further develop flavour and aroma. After roasting and cooling, the seeds are shelled. The shells and scraps are normally sold for animal feed. The meat (known as nibs), which is made up of about 50 percent cocoa butter, are then ground to produce chocolate liquor. A proportion of the liquor is cooled and processed to extract a proportion of the cocoa butter, leaving behind a compressed mass which is the source of cocoa powder.

Types of Chocolate

Chocolate can be divided into four broad usage types: cooking chocolate, eating chocolate, cocoa powders and other chocolate products. The quality of chocolate is based on the percentage of cocoa butter, which should always be listed on the label of the product, so check this before purchasing. The higher the percentage of cocoa butter content, the better the chocolate and higher the quality of your finished product.

EATING CHOCOLATE

Eating chocolate comes in a wide variety of flavours and fillings. It is generally sweeter than cooking chocolate, and is not as suitable for cooking. The amount of sugar added depends on the formula of the individual manufacturer. It is broadly divided into the following types: bittersweet, dark, milk and white.

BITTERSWEET CHOCOLATE

Bittersweet chocolate has a high percentage of cocoa liquor – 70 percent or above.

DARK CHOCOLATE

This is chocolate with a relatively high proportion of cocoa liquor, but under 70 percent of cocoa liquor. In Britain this is known as plain chocolate, and in America as semi-sweet chocolate.

MILK CHOCOLATE

This is dark chocolate with more sugar and dried milk solids added. Widely used for chocolate bars and confectionery.

WHITE CHOCOLATE

This is white-coloured 'chocolate' which lacks chocolate liquor, so technically is not real chocolate. Contains cocoa butter with added sugar, milk and flavourings. Should not be substituted for chocolate in recipes.

COOKING CHOCOLATE

Cooking chocolate generally has a higher proportion of cocoa butter and a lower proportion of sugar than eating chocolate. It is available in both dark and milk varieties as well as the varieties listed below.

COMMERCIAL COATING OR COUVERTURE CHOCOLATE

The highest grade of cooking chocolate, used by professional confectioners to make high-quality sweets and cake decorations, including curls, ruffles and other garnishes. It has more cacao butter than regular cooking chocolate, which allows it to melt and spread well, but makes it trickier for a non-professional to handle.

SOLID UNSWEETENED CHOCOLATE

This chocolate is bitter and unsuitable for eating. Professional chefs often use it in cooking as it gives them better control of the sugar content and flavour of the product.

CHOCOLATE CHIPS/BUTTONS/BUDS /MORSELS

This is chocolate sold as small disks which contain a lower percentage of cocoa butter (about 29 percent) than chocolate bars. This helps them retain their shape when baked in biscuits and muffins. Available in dark, milk and white chocolate varieties.

CHOCOLATE MELTS

Chocolate sold as small disks especially designed for non-professionals, as they are easy to work with when melted.

COMPOUND CHOCOLATE

Compound chocolate, also called chocolate coating or compound coating chocolate, is an imitation product designed to replace high-quality chocolate in cooking. It can be purchased in block or disk form and in milk and dark varieties. Compound chocolate is made from a vegetable oil base combined with sugar, milk solids and flavouring. It contains cocoa powder but little or no cocoa butter and is easy to melt. It does not require tempering (see page 9) and so is the easiest form for beginners to work with.

INSTANT COCOA PRODUCTS

These products usually contain lecithin or other emulsifiers that make cocoa easier to dissolve in cold liquids.

COCOA POWDERS AND DRINKING COCOA

Powdered cocoa is produced by pressing enough cocoa butter out of the chocolate liquor to leave a press cake with a content of 10–25 percent cocoa butter. It is used to make a variety of subsidiary products.

DUTCH COCOA POWDER

This cocoa powder is produced by a Dutch method using an alkaline. The result is a smooth, rich and milder flavour than natural cocoa powder.

UNSWEETENED COCOA POWDER

This cocoa powder is less alkaline than Dutch cocoa, so care must be taken if substituting for Dutch cocoa in recipes. You may need to adjust levels of baking powder and bicarbonate of soda to suit.

DRINKING CHOCOLATE (POWDER)

This powder has milk solids and sugar added to cocoa powder to make it more palatable for drinking. It will not dissolve easily in cold liquids.

OTHER CHOCOLATE PRODUCTS

- Chocolate-flavoured syrup

- Sugar or corn syrup and cocoa blended with preservatives, emulsifiers and flavourings. Used for a topping for ice cream and desserts.

Basic Techniques

STORING CHOCOLATE

Chocolate should be stored in a dry, airy place at a temperature of about 16°C. If stored in unsuitable conditions, the cocoa butter in chocolate may rise to the surface, leaving a white film or 'bloom'. A similar discolouration occurs when water condenses on the surface.

This can happen to refrigerated chocolates that have been too loosely wrapped. Chocolate affected in this way is still suitable for melting, but not for grating.

MELTING CHOCOLATE

Chocolate melts more rapidly if broken into small pieces. The melting process should occur slowly since chocolate scorches if overheated. To melt chocolate, place the chocolate in the top of a double saucepan or in a bowl set over a saucepan of simmering water and heat, stirring, until chocolate melts and becomes smooth.

Alternatively, chocolate can be melted in the microwave. To melt 375g chocolate, break it into small pieces and place in a microwavable glass or ceramic bowl or jug and cook on High (100 percent) for 1 minute. Stir. If the chocolate is not completely melted cook for 30–45 seconds longer. When melting chocolate in the microwave you should be aware that it holds its shape and it is important to stir it frequently so that it does not burn.

- The container in which the chocolate is being melted should be kept uncovered and completely dry. Covering could cause condensation and just one drop of water will ruin the chocolate.

- Chocolate 'seizes' if it is overheated, or if it comes into contact with water or steam. Seizing results in the chocolate tightening and becoming a thick mass that will not melt. To rescue seized chocolate, stir in a little cream or vegetable oil until the chocolate becomes smooth again.

Making Decorations

The recipes in this book call for a variety of chocolate decorations, such as the ones described below.

CHOCOLATE LEAVES

To make chocolate leaves, choose non-poisonous, fresh, stiff leaves with raised veins. When picking, retain as much stem as possible. Wash leaves, then dry well on absorbent kitchen paper. Brush the underside of the leaves with melted chocolate and allow to set at room temperature. When set, carefully peel away leaf. Use one leaf to decorate an individual dessert, or a make a number and use to decorate a large dessert or cake.

CHOCOLATE CASES

To make chocolate cases for filled chocolates, quarter-fill a mould with melted chocolate and tap mould to remove any air bubbles. Brush chocolate evenly up sides of mould to make a shell, then freeze for 2 minutes or until set. Larger chocolate cases to hold desserts can also be made in this way using foil-lined individual metal flan tins, brioche or muffin tins as moulds. When set, remove from tins and fill with dessert filling such as mousse or a flavoured cream.

CHOCOLATE CARAQUE

Chocolate caraque is a layer of chocolate scrolls or flakes, used for example to decorate a Black Forest Cake. This is made by spreading a layer of melted chocolate over a marble, granite or ceramic work surface. Allow the chocolate to set at room temperature. Then, holding a metal pastry scraper or a large knife at a 45° angle, slowly push it along the work surface away from you to form the chocolate into cylinders. If chocolate shavings form, then the chocolate is too cold and the chocolate is best to start again.

CHOCOLATE CURLS OR SHAVINGS

Chocolate curls are made from chocolate that is at room temperature. To make shavings, you need to use chilled chocolate. Using a vegetable peeler, shave the sides of the chocolate. Whether curls or shavings form depends on the temperature of the chocolate.

PIPED CHOCOLATE DECORATIONS

You can use piped chocolate decorations to decorate cakes, pastries and desserts and they are quick and easy to make. Trace a simple design onto a sheet of paper. Tape a sheet of baking or greaseproof paper to your work surface and slide the drawings under the paper. Place melted chocolate into a paper or material piping bag (see instructions page 11) and, following the tracings, pipe thin lines. Allow to set at room temperature and then carefully remove, using a metal spatula. If you are not going to use these decorations immediately, store them in an airtight container in a cool place.

MAKING A PAPER PIPING BAG

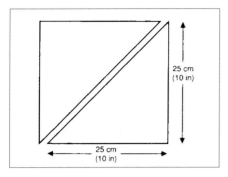
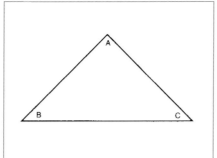
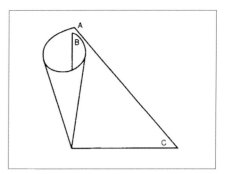

1 Cut a 25cm square of waxed paper.

2 Cut the square in half diagonally to form two triangles.

3 To make the piping bag, place the paper triangles on top of each other and mark the three corners A, B and C.

4 Fold corner B around and inside corner A.

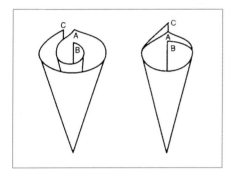
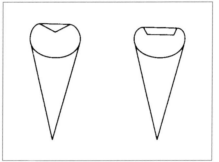

5 Bring corner C around the outside of the bag until it fits exactly behind corner A. At this stage all three corners should be together and the point closed.

6 Fold corner A over two or three times to hold the bag together.

7 Snip the point off the bag and drop into icing nozzle. The piping bag can be used without a nozzle for writing and outlines, in which case only the very tip of the point should be snipped off the bag.

FILLING A PIPING BAG

Spoon chocolate or icing into the bag to half-full. Fold about 1cm of the bag over then fold over again. Fold the tips towards the centre and press your thumb on the join to force the chocolate or icing out.

USING A PIPING BAG

Grip the piping bag near the top with the folded or twisted end held between the thumb and fingers. Guide the bag with your free hand. Right-handed people should decorate from left to right, while left-handers need to decorate from right to left, except when piping writing.

The appearance of your piping will be directly affected by how you squeeze and relax your grip on the piping bag, that is, the pressure you apply and the steadiness of that pressure. The pressure should be so consistent that you can move the bag in a free and easy glide with just the right amount of chocolate or icing flowing from the nozzle. A little practice will soon have you feeling confident.

dreamy desserts

Rich Chocolate Soufflés

(see photograph on page 12)

1 tablespoon melted butter

100g raw sugar, plus 1 tablespoon, for sprinkling

100g bittersweet chocolate, broken into pieces

2 tablespoons orange juice

2 medium eggs, separated

½ teaspoon finely grated orange zest

pinch of salt

cocoa powder for dusting (optional)

1 Preheat oven to 190°C. Grease the sides of four individual 115ml ramekin dishes or ovenproof soufflé dishes with the butter. Sprinkle 1 tablespoon of sugar equally between the dishes, dust the sides and shake out any excess. Preheat the oven and place a baking sheet in it.

2 Heat the chocolate and orange juice in a bowl over a pan of simmering water, until the chocolate has melted and the mixture is smooth. Remove from the heat allow to cool slightly and stir in the egg yolks with the orange zest and half the sugar.

3 Whisk the egg whites in a large bowl with the salt until they form stiff peaks, then slowly whisk in the remaining sugar. Fold a quarter of the egg whites into the chocolate followed by the remaining egg whites. Spoon the mixture into the dishes and place in the oven on the hot baking sheet. Cook for 12–14 minutes until well risen and just set. Dust with cocoa powder and serve.

Serves 4

Note: These individual light chocolate soufflés have just a hint of orange. If you think cream is too sinful, try serving them with a raspberry sauce (see page 85).

Dark Chocolate Ice Cream

(see photograph opposite)

1⅕ cups full-fat milk

60g soft dark brown sugar

30g cocoa powder, sifted

100g dark chocolate, broken into small chunks

145g carton thickened or pure full cream

fresh mint to decorate

1 Place the milk and sugar in a saucepan and bring to the boil, then quickly stir in the cocoa powder and add the chocolate chunks. Remove from the heat and stir until the chocolate melts. Set aside to cool for 20 minutes.

2 Whip the cream until it forms soft peaks. Fold it into the warm chocolate mixture and stir gently until thoroughly combined. Pour into a freezer container and freeze for 4 hours or until firm, whisking the mixture every hour. Scoop into dessert bowls and serve, decorated with the mint leaves.

Serves 4

Note: Home-made ice cream is delicious, and this is one of the best. You can make it a week or two in advance, but as it freezes very hard, you will need to defrost it for 20 minutes before serving, to let it soften.

Ice Cream Christmas Pudding

1 litre chocolate ice cream, softened

125g glacé apricots, chopped

125g glacé cherries, chopped

125g glacé pears, chopped

90g sultanas

75g raisins, chopped

2 tablespoons rum

1 Place ice cream, apricots, cherries, pears, sultanas, raisins and rum in a bowl and mix to combine. Pour into an oiled and lined 6-cup capacity pudding basin.

2 Freeze for 3 hours or until firm. Slice pudding and serve with rum custard.

Serves 8

Note: To help release the pudding from the mould, briefly hold a warm damp tea towel around the outside of the basin.

Sweet Little Bonfires

15g dried mixed fruit

60g cornflakes

100g shredded wheat biscuits, crushed (about 4 biscuits)

100g candied cherries, chopped

¾ cup condensed milk

150g desiccated coconut

150g milk chocolate

1 Preheat the oven to 160°C. Line 3 baking trays with baking or rice paper. Combine the dried mixed fruit, cornflakes, biscuits, cherries, condensed milk and coconut in a large bowl. Press the mixture into little mounds and place them on the baking trays, spacing them evenly. Bake for 15 minutes or until golden and crisp.

2 Meanwhile, melt the chocolate in a bowl over a saucepan of simmering water. Remove the 'bonfires' from the oven and leave for 2 minutes to cool slightly. Drizzle over the melted chocolate and cool for a further 1–2 minutes before serving.

Serves 4

Note: These can be made by children without too much supervision. But be warned, they'll disappear faster than crackers at a bonfire night!

Chocolate Crème Brulée

500g plum pudding

4½ cups pure cream

100g caster sugar

250g bittersweet chocolate

8 large egg yolks

1 tablespoon Dutch cocoa powder

100g pure icing sugar

1   Preheat oven to 150°C. Cut the plum pudding into tiny cubes and sprinkle cubes equally over the bases of 12 ovenproof ramekins.

2   Place a large stainless steel bowl over a pot of simmering water and whisk the cream and sugar together gently (in the bowl) until the sugar has dissolved. Add the chocolate, broken into small pieces, and continue mixing until the chocolate has dissolved. Remove from the heat.

3   In a separate bowl, whisk the egg yolks until they form a smooth ribbon. Mix the whisked egg yolks, chocolate mixture and Dutch cocoa until thoroughly combined. Pour this custard mixture into a jug and divide between the prepared ramekins.

4   Place the ramekins into a large ovenproof baking dish and add hot water to reach halfway up the outsides. Bake for 30 minutes (or until set). Remove the baking dish and take the ramekins out of the water bath. Chill the custards for at least 2 hours (or overnight).

5   Before serving, sieve the icing sugar generously over the custards. Caramelise the sugar under a grill until bubbling and golden. Alternatively, you can buy a small blow-torch from a good kitchenware shop and use this to caramelise the sugar. If grilling, watch carefully to avoid burning the sugar.

Serves 12

Note: Chocolate crème brulée is one of the most seductive desserts you can make. The rich chocolate flavours and the smooth texture of the custard is enhanced by the crisp toffee coating. Don't wait for Christmas to enjoy this lovely recipe.

Frozen Maple-Nut Parfait

6 egg yolks

220g caster sugar

125ml water

125ml maple syrup

600ml double cream

100g macadamia nuts, finely chopped

100g white chocolate, chopped

extra maple syrup

1 Place egg yolks in a bowl and beat until thick and pale.

2 To make a sugar syrup, place sugar and water in a saucepan and heat over a low heat, stirring, until sugar dissolves. Bring mixture to the boil and boil until mixture thickens and reaches soft-ball stage or 118°C on a sugar thermometer. Allow to cool.

3 Gradually beat sugar syrup and maple syrup into beaten egg yolks and continue beating until mixture cools. Place cream in a bowl and beat until soft peaks form. Fold cream, macadamia nuts and chocolate into egg mixture.

4 Pour mixture into an aluminium foil-lined 15 x 25cm loaf tin and freeze for 5 hours or until firm.

5 Turn parfait onto a serving plate, remove foil, cut into slices and drizzle with maple syrup.

Serves 8

Note: This light and luscious frozen Italian dessert is perfect served with a garnish of fresh fruit and perhaps some almond-flavoured biscotti.

Chocolate Hazelnut Fondue

(see photograph opposite, back)

¼ cup orange juice

2 tablespoons chocolate hazelnut
  spread

375g chocolate melts

1 cup cream

fresh fruit

1   Place juice, chocolate hazelnut spread and chocolate melts in a microwave-proof bowl. Microwave on high for 1½ minutes. Stir until combined and smooth. Add cream and mix to combine. Pour into a fondue pot and place over low flame. Prepare fruit, peeling, segmenting and slicing as necessary. Use to dip into fondue.

Serves 4–6

Chocolate Custard Flan

(see photograph opposite, front left)

1½ cups plain flour

¼ cup cocoa

¼ cup sugar

125g butter

1 egg

1 tablespoon water

chocolate shavings to decorate

FILLING

100g cooking chocolate

2 eggs

1 cup milk

1 teaspoon vanilla essence

1   Sift flour and cocoa together. Add sugar. Chop butter into small pieces and rub with fingertips into flour mixture. Mix in egg and water. Form dough into a ball. Rest pastry for 20 minutes in refrigerator.

2   Roll pastry out and line a 20cm flan dish with it. Pour filling into flan dish and bake at 180°C for 25–30 minutes or until custard has set. Decorate with chocolate shavings.

FILLING

1   Melt chocolate and cool slightly. Beat eggs into chocolate one at a time. Add milk and vanilla essence and stir to combine.

Serves 6

Spiced Chocolate Bread and Butter Pudding

(see photograph opposite, front right)

6 spiced buns

60g butter

3 eggs

4 cups milk

¼ cup sugar

1 teaspoon vanilla essence

125g cooking chocolate

1   Cut buns into 1cm slices. Butter slices. Beat eggs, milk, sugar and vanilla essence in a bowl. Break chocolate into pieces. Place a layer of bread, butter-side down, in a 21 x 26cm ovenproof dish.

2   Divide chocolate into three. Scatter first measure of chocolate over buns. Place a second layer of bread over chocolate, butter-side down. Scatter second amount of chocolate over. Place remaining layer of buns, butter-side down, and scatter remaining chocolate over.

3   Pour egg mixture over buns and chocolate layers. Stand for 30 minutes. Place ovenproof dish into a baking dish with warm water to come halfway up sides of the oven-proof dish. Bake at 160°C for 1–1½ hours.

Serves 8–10

Caramel-Walnut Petits Fours

250g white sugar

90g brown sugar

2 cups double cream

1 cup light corn or golden syrup

60g butter, chopped

½ teaspoon bicarbonate of soda

155g chopped walnuts

1 tablespoon vanilla essence

CHOCOLATE ICING

375g dark or milk chocolate, melted

2 teaspoons vegetable oil

1   Place sugar, brown sugar, cream, corn or golden syrup and butter in a saucepan and heat over a low heat, stirring constantly, until sugar dissolves. As sugar crystals form on sides of pan, brush them with a wet pastry brush to stop the syrup crystallising.

2   Bring syrup to the boil and stir in bicarbonate of soda. Reduce heat and simmer until syrup reaches the hard-ball stage or 120°C on a sugar thermometer.

3   Stir in walnuts and vanilla essence and pour mixture into a greased and foil-lined 20cm square cake tin. Set aside at room temperature for 5 hours or until caramel sets.

4   Remove caramel from tin and cut into 2cm squares.

5   To make icing, combine melted chocolate and oil. Half-dip caramels in melted chocolate, place on greaseproof paper and leave to set.

Makes 40

Note: For easy removal of the caramel from the tin, allow the foil lining to overhang the tin on two opposite sides to form handles for lifting.

Tuile Cups with White Chocolate

TUILES

125g butter, melted

4 egg whites

2 tablespoons milk

125g plain flour

140g caster sugar

60g flaked almonds

WHITE CHOCOLATE FILLING

250g white chocolate, broken
  into pieces

60g butter, chopped

¼ cup single cream

1 Preheat oven to 160°C. To make tuiles, place butter, egg whites, milk, flour and sugar in a bowl and beat until smooth.

2 Place 2 teaspoons of mixture on a lightly greased baking tray and spread out to make a 10cm round. Repeat with remaining mixture leaving 10cm between each tuile. Sprinkle with almonds and bake for 3–5 minutes or until edges of tuiles are golden. Using a spatula, carefully remove tuiles from trays and place over a small upturned strainer. Press gently to form into cup shapes, then allow to cool and harden before removing from strainer.

3 To make filling, place chocolate, butter and cream in a heatproof bowl simmering water and heat over, stirring, until mixture is smooth. Remove bowl from pan and set aside until mixture thickens slightly. Beat mixture until light and thick. Spoon mixture into a piping bag and pipe into tuile cups.

Makes 28

Note: These very thin and brittle biscuits were named 'tuiles' (tiles) because they replicated the shape of old fashioned French roofing tiles, and are traditionally made with almonds. This version uses a tuile recipe to create delicate cups to hold the rich white chocolate filling.

Banana Mousse

1 tablespoon gelatine

¼ cup boiling water

500g ripe bananas

60g sugar

1 tablespoon lemon juice

1 cup double cream

⅓ cup coconut milk

100g dark chocolate, melted

1 Place gelatine and boiling water in a bowl and stir until gelatine dissolves. Set aside to cool.

2 Place bananas, sugar and lemon juice in a food processor and process until smooth. Stir gelatine mixture into banana mixture.

3 Place cream and coconut milk in a bowl and beat until soft peaks form. Fold cream mixture into banana mixture.

4 Spoon mousse into six serving glasses. Pour on melted chocolate divided equally between glasses and swirl with a skewer. Refrigerate for 2 hours or until set.

Serves 6

Note: Dried banana chips of fresh mint leaves make an attractive garnish.

Chocolate Mousse with Fresh Berries

170g bittersweet chocolate, chopped

2 teaspoons powdered gelatine

¼ cup water

100g reduced-fat ricotta

1 cup reduced-fat vanilla custard

4 egg whites

300g mixed fresh berries (strawberries, raspberries, blueberries)

1   Put the chocolate in an ovenproof bowl over a pot of simmering water, making sure the base of the bowl does not come in contact with the water and that no water touches the chocolate. Stir over a low heat until the chocolate melts then set aside to cool slightly.

2   Put the gelatine and water into a small pot and stir over a low heat until the gelatine dissolves and the liquid is clear. Remove from the heat and allow to cool slightly.

3   Beat the ricotta and custard together until smooth. Press through a sieve to remove any lumps. Beat egg whites until light and fluffy, then set aside.

4   Fold the gelatin and chocolate into the ricotta mix. Then fold in the beaten egg whites. Spoon the mousse into 6 x 115ml ramekins or mugs, cover and refrigerate for 1 hour or until set. Serve with the berries.

Serves 6

Quick Chocolate Mousse

(see photograph opposite, back)

150g cooking chocolate

4 eggs

1¼ cups single cream

3 tablespoons icing sugar

fresh fruit to decorate

1 Break chocolate into a saucepan and melt over a gentle heat or over hot water. Separate eggs and mix yolks into melted chocolate. Beat until smooth. Beat cream until thick. Fold cream into chocolate mixture.

2 Beat egg whites until stiff. Beat in icing sugar, beating until thick. Fold chocolate mixture into egg whites. Pour into individual serving dishes or one bowl. Refrigerate until firm. Decorate with fresh fruit.

Serves 6

Chocolate Cherry Clafouti

(see photograph opposite, centre)

2 cups drained, canned, pitted cherries

1 cup milk

3 eggs

½ teaspoon almond essence

¼ cup icing sugar

¼ cup plain flour

¼ cup cocoa

1 tablespoon icing sugar

1 Spread cherries over the base of a lightly greased, 4-cup capacity ovenproof dish. Lightly beat milk, eggs and almond essence together. Sift in icing sugar, flour and cocoa and whisk until smooth. Pour over cherries.

2 Bake at 180°C for 45–50 minutes or until clafouti is set. Sprinkle with icing sugar and serve.

Serves 6

Note: Change the fruit if cherries aren't your favourite or are unavailable.

Chocolate Nut Torte

(see photograph opposite, front)

1½ cup roasted almonds

250g cooking chocolate

1½ cups dates

6 egg whites

½ cup caster sugar

½ teaspoon ground cinnamon

1 Chop almonds, chocolate and dates roughly. Beat egg whites until stiff peaks form. Slowly add caster sugar and cinnamon. Fold in almonds, chocolate and dates.

2 Line a 23cm cake tin with foil and pour in cake mixture. Bake at 180°C for 45–50 minutes until firm to touch. Cool in oven with door slightly open. When cold, place on a serving platter, cover and refrigerate overnight.

Serves 10–12

Note: This torte is best served chilled, as it will crumble if cut warm. It will keep refrigerated for several days.

Chocolate and Orange Mousse

1 tablespoon arrowroot flour

1⅗ cups orange juice

grated zest of 1 orange

3 tablespoons caster sugar

200g milk chocolate, broken into pieces

2–3 tablespoons orange liqueur or
  brandy

butter for greasing

½ cup double cream

¾ cup heavy cream

fresh strawberries to decorate

1 Mix together the arrowroot flour and 3 tablespoons of the orange juice until
   smooth. Place the rest of the orange juice, the zest and sugar in a small
   saucepan and bring to the boil, then simmer for minute or until the sugar has
   dissolved. Stir in the arrowroot mixture and bring back to the boil, stirring
   constantly. Boil for a few seconds, stirring, until the mixture is glossy and
   slightly thickened.

2 Add the chocolate to the orange mixture, then remove from the heat and
   stir until the chocolate has melted. Stir in the liqueur, then cover the mixture
   with a round of buttered baking paper to prevent a skin forming. Cool for
   30 minutes.

3 Whip the whipping and cream together until the mixture forms soft peaks.
   Gently fold into the cooled chocolate mixture. Transfer to 6 serving dishes,
   cover and place in the fridge for 2 hours. Remove from the fridge
   15 minutes before serving and decorate with strawberries.

Serves 6

Chocolate Hot Cakes with Raspberry Coulis

1½ cups plain flour

2 teaspoons baking powder

2 tablespoons sugar

2 eggs

1 cup low-fat single cream

¼ cup chocolate sauce

RASPBERRY COULIS

1 cup fresh or thawed frozen
  raspberries

2 tablespoons sugar

1 tablespoon lemon juice

1 Sift flour and baking powder into a bowl. Stir in sugar. Mix eggs, cream and chocolate sauce together.

2 Make a well in the centre of the dry ingredients and pour in egg mixture. Stir to combine.

3 Cook half-cupfuls of mixture in a hot, greased frying pan, turning to cook both sides. Serve with raspberry coulis and extra chocolate sauce.

RASPBERRY COULIS

1 Place raspberries, sugar and lemon juice in the bowl of a food processor and process to combine.

Makes 5

Note: Try these for a classy weekend breakfast.

Chocolate French Toast with Cinnamon Bananas

2 eggs

½ cup milk

¼ cup chocolate sauce

8 x 2cm-thick diagonally cut slices
stale baguette

50g butter

CINNAMON BANANAS

4 small bananas

50g butter

3 tablespoons brown sugar

1 teaspoon ground cinnamon

1   Lightly beat eggs, milk and chocolate sauce together until combined. Soak baguette slices in this.

2   Heat butter in a large frying pan until it stops frothing. Place baguette slices in hot butter and cook each side for 1–2 minutes or until egg mixture is set and baguette is lightly golden. Allow two pieces of French toast per serving.

3   Arrange on a plate with cinnamon bananas and drizzle any syrup left in banana pan over the top.

CINNAMON BANANAS

1   Peel bananas and cut in half lengthwise.

2   Melt butter in a frying pan. Add brown sugar and cook until bubbling. Mix in cinnamon. Add bananas, turning carefully to coat both sides in butter mixture. Cook for 1 minute each side.

Serves 4

Tim's Vacherin

4 egg whites

1 cup caster sugar

1 teaspoon vanilla essence

2 litres vanilla ice cream

2 teaspoons vanilla essence

½ cup chopped roasted hazelnuts

prepared chocolate sauce

½ cup whipped cream

fruit for decoration

1   Beat egg whites until stiff. Gradually add sugar, beating until all sugar is added and mixture is smooth, stiff and glossy. Beat in first measure of vanilla essence.

2   Mark circles about 7cm in diameter on a piece of baking paper. Place paper, marked side down, on a baking tray. Spread 2 tablespoonfuls of mixture on baking paper in circles to make 21 round, flat meringues.

3   Bake at 150°C for 40 minutes or until meringues are crisp and dry. Soften ice cream and divide in half. Mix second measure of vanilla essence into one half and hazelnuts into the other. Freeze until firm.

4   To serve, place a meringue round on a plate. Top with a scoop of vanilla ice cream, another meringue round, a scoop of hazelnut ice cream and another meringue round. Pour chocolate sauce and whipped cream over. Decorate with fruit.

Serves 7

Chocolate Pâté

200g cooking chocolate

50g butter

2 egg yolks

1 Melt chocolate and butter in a saucepan over a low heat.

2 Mix in egg yolks. Remove from heat.

3 Pour mixture into an 11 x 7cm loaf tin, with baking paper covering the sides and bottom of tin, or into individual dishes. Refrigerate until firm.

4 Serve with sweet biscuits, raspberry jam and raspberries.

Serves 6

Note: If raspberries are out of season, use other fresh or drained canned fruit with a jam to match. This is a different idea for dessert and great with coffee.

Chocolate Pear Crumble

425g can pears

1 teaspoon mixed spice

½ cup chocolate melts

½ cup brown sugar

½ cup rolled oats

1 tablespoon cocoa

½ cup plain flour

75g butter

1 Drain pears and cut into 1cm slices. Place in a 4-cup capacity ovenproof dish and sprinkle mixed spice over.

2 Mix chocolate melts through. Place brown sugar, rolled oats, cocoa and flour in a bowl. Melt butter and mix into flour mixture. Scatter mixture over pears.

3 Bake at 180°C for 25–30 minutes.

Serves 4

Chocolate and Date Logs

(see photograph opposite)

250g packet malt biscuits

½ cup roasted chopped walnuts

2 cups chopped dates

½ cup desiccated coconut

½ cup chocolate melts

50g butter

¼ cup golden syrup

1 cup sweetened condensed milk

1 tablespoon cocoa

¾ cup toasted sesame seeds

1 Place biscuits in a food processor and chop roughly.

2 Place in a bowl with walnuts, dates, coconut and chocolate melts. Melt butter, golden syrup, condensed milk and cocoa together in a saucepan, stirring until just combined. Cool. Stir into biscuit mixture.

3 Place bowl in refrigerator for 1 hour.

4 Break off tablespoonfuls and roll into 4cm cylindrical shapes. Roll in toasted sesame seeds. Store in refrigerator.

Makes 60

Chocolate Macadamia Truffles

(see photograph opposite)

300g packet cooking chocolate

1 cup macadamia nuts

½ cup sticky raisins

½ cup apricot jam

50g butter

1 Chop half the chocolate roughly and place in a food processor with nuts, raisins and jam. Process to combine but not to a paste.

2 Roll tablespoonfuls of mixture into balls.

3 Melt remaining chocolate and butter together and dip truffle balls into this. Place on a wire rack until set.

Makes 22

biscuits and slices

Hazelnut Snowballs

200g white chocolate, broken
  into pieces

45g butter, chopped

¼ cup double cream

1 tablespoon hazelnut-flavoured liqueur
  (optional)

125g hazelnuts, toasted with
  skins removed

60g desiccated coconut

1 Place chocolate, butter, cream and liqueur, if using, in a heatproof bowl set over a saucepan of simmering water and heat, stirring, until mixture is smooth. Remove bowl from pan and set aside to cool slightly.

2 Stir chocolate mixture until thick and pliable. Roll tablespoons of mixture into balls. Press a hazelnut into the centre of each ball and roll to enclose nut. Roll balls in coconut and refrigerate for 1 hour or until firm.

Makes 4

Chocolate Raspberry Brownies

1 cup plain flour

2 teaspoons bicarbonate of soda

¾ cup cocoa powder

2 eggs, lightly beaten

1¼ cups caster sugar

1 teaspoon vanilla essence

1½ tablespoons sunflower oil

200g reduced-fat vanilla yoghurt

½ cup apple purée

200g fresh or frozen raspberries

pure icing sugar, to dust

fresh berries, to serve

1 Preheat the oven to 180°C. Grease and line the base and sides of a 30 x 20cm baking tin with baking paper.

2 Sift the flour, bicarbonate of soda and cocoa into a large bowl and make a well in the centre.

3 Whisk together the eggs, sugar, vanilla, oil and yoghurt in a large jug. Add to the flour mixture and mix until smooth. Fold through the apple purée and raspberries.

4 Spoon the mixture into the prepared tin and bake for 30 minutes or until a skewer comes out clean when inserted in the centre. Allow to cool for 5 minutes in the tin before turning out onto a wire rack to cool completely.

5 Cut into 16 squares and dust with icing sugar. Serve cool or warm with extra fresh berries and reduced-fat ice cream.

Makes 16

Chocolate Almond Balls

½ cup pure cream

125g bittersweet chocolate, chopped

1 tablespoon butter

60g almonds, finely chopped, toasted

30g puffed rice cereal, crushed

1 Place the cream and chocolate in a saucepan and cook over a low heat, stirring, until the chocolate melts. Remove the pan from the heat and set aside to cool slightly. Stir in the butter, cover and chill in refrigerator.

2 Using an electric mixer, beat the chocolate mixture until soft peaks form. Return to the refrigerator until firm.

3 Place the almonds and rice cereal in a bowl and mix to combine. Shape teaspoons of the chocolate mixture into balls and roll in the almond mixture. Store in an airtight container in the refrigerator.

Makes 24

Note: Served with coffee this uncooked biscuit makes a delicious after-dinner treat.

Chocolate and Date-Stuffed Baklava

SYRUP

1 cup white sugar

½ cup brown sugar

⅔ cup water

pinch of ground allspice

pinch of ground ginger

pinch of ground cloves

FILLING

200g walnuts, toasted

100g almonds, toasted

170g bittersweet chocolate, chopped

170g dates, stones removed

2 tablespoons sugar

1 tablespoon cinnamon

1 egg, beaten

24 sheets filo pastry

125g butter

60g milk chocolate, chopped

1 cup pure cream, if desired

1   Preheat the oven to 190°C. To make the syrup, bring all the syrup ingredients to a simmer in a small saucepan, stirring until the sugar dissolves. Continue simmering for 1 minute then cool completely.

2   To make the filling, combine the walnuts, almonds, chocolate, dates, sugar and cinnamon in a food processor and process until roughly chopped. (Don't overprocess.) Transfer the mixture to a bowl and mix in the egg.

3   Butter a 30 x 20 cm metal baking dish. Unwrap the filo pastry and place it on a flat work surface under a damp cloth. Melt the butter.

4   Place 1 sheet of pastry in front of you then brush lightly with butter, paying particular attention to the edges of the sheet of pastry. Place another sheet of pastry on top of the first, repeating the buttering. Repeat with 6 more sheets so that you have 8 in all. Fold this pastry stack in half to make it fit the prepared baking tin, place it neatly in the tin. Sprinkle half the prepared nut filling over the pastry, making sure the coverage is even.

5   Repeat the buttering and folding with 8 more sheets of pastry and place the folded pastry over the nuts. Add the remaining nut filling over the second stack of pastry. Repeat the buttering and folding with the remaining sheets of pastry and place over the nut filling.

6   Using a sharp knife, score the pastry into four long strips, then cut these strips diagonally to form 24 diamond-shaped pieces of baklava. Pour any remaining butter over the pastry, then bake for 40 minutes, until the top of the pastry is deep golden brown. Pour the syrup over the baklava then allow to cool completely.

7   Grate the chocolate over the baklava, then allow to stand at room temperature overnight. Serve with whipped fresh cream (if desired).

Makes 24

Double Coconut Chocolate Cream Biscuits

125g butter

¾ cup brown sugar

1 teaspoon vanilla essence

2 eggs

1 cup coconut

1½ cups plain flour

2 tablespoons cocoa powder

1 teaspoon baking powder

COCONUT CHOCOLATE FILLING

2 tablespoons butter

1½ cups pure icing sugar

1 tablespoon cocoa powder

3 tablespoons coconut cream powder

1–2 tablespoons water

1 Preheat oven to 180°C. Melt butter in a saucepan large enough to mix all the ingredients. Remove from the heat and mix in sugar and vanilla essence.

2 Add eggs and beat with a wooden spoon until combined. Add coconut and sift in flour, cocoa and baking powder. Mix until combined.

3 Roll teaspoons of mixture into balls. Place on an oven tray, allowing room to spread. Flatten with a fork.

4 Bake for 12–15 minutes or until cooked. Cool on a wire rack.

5 When cold, sandwich together with Coconut Chocolate Filling.

COCONUT CHOCOLATE FILLING

1 Melt butter. Place icing sugar, cocoa and coconut cream powder in a bowl, mixing to combine. Mix in butter and enough water to make a spreadable filling.

Makes 12

Note: Coconut is high in saturated fat. If you would prefer to avoid this in your diet but can't resist the look of these delicious biscuits, substituting crushed cornflakes for the coconut in the biscuits, and omit the coconut cream powder from the filling.

Choc-Filled Butterscotch Pecan Thins

370g unsalted butter, softened

1 cup firmly packed light brown sugar

1 large egg

1½ teaspoons vanilla essence

1½ cups plain flour

3⁄4 teaspoon baking powder

½ teaspoon salt

about 48 pecan halves

GANACHE

100g bittersweet chocolate

100ml double cream

1   Using an electric mixer, cream the butter with the sugar until the mixture is light and fluffy then beat in the egg and the vanilla.

2   Sift together the flour, baking powder and salt and mix the dough until it is firm enough to handle. Halve the dough then roll each half into a 15cm long log. Wrap each log in a piece of baking paper or plastic wrap, using it to help you roll a tight and even log.

3   Chill the logs, wrapped in the paper or plastic, for 4 hours or overnight.

4   Preheat the oven to 180°C.

5   Cut the logs into 5mm thick slices with a sharp knife and arrange the slices on lightly greased baking trays, leaving plenty of room for spreading. Before baking, press a pecan half onto each cookie.

6   Bake the biscuits in batches in the middle of the oven for 10 to 12 minutes or until golden brown, then let them cool on the baking trays for 1 minute.

7   Repeat the cutting and baking with the remaining dough then transfer all the biscuits to racks and let them cool completely.

8   To make the ganache, break the chocolate into small pieces and heat the cream until almost boiling. Pour the hot cream over the chocolate and allow the chocolate to melt slowly. After 5 minutes, mix the chocolate cream mixture until the chocolate has melted and the mixture is thick and smooth.

9   Leave the ganache at room temperature until it is spreadable and cool. Then fill a piping bag and pipe or spoon a small mound of ganache onto half of the biscuits. Gently press another cookie onto the chocolate, to spread the filling.

10 Allow the biscuits and filling to cool and set, then serve. Can be stored in the fridge for up to 5 days.

Makes 30

Note: A ganache is a filling or glaze made of pure cream, chocolate, and/or other flavourings. It is often used to sandwich the layers of gourmet chocolate cakes. A ganache is made by pouring hot cream over chopped up chocolate and whipping the mixture until the chocolate melts and the mixture becomes thick and stiff.

Truffle Easter Eggs

TRUFFLE EASTER EGGS

125g dark chocolate, tempered

TRUFFLE FILLING

½ cup double cream

250g milk chocolate

1 tablespoon golden syrup

1 Place a spoonful of tempered dark chocolate (see page 9) in a small Easter egg mould and use a small paintbrush to evenly coat the mould. Freeze for 2 minutes or until chocolate sets. Repeat with remaining chocolate to make 32 shells.

2 To make filling, place cream in a saucepan and bring to the boil. Remove pan from heat, add milk chocolate and stir until chocolate is melted and mixture is smooth. Stir in golden syrup and chill for 20 minutes or until mixture is thick enough to pipe.

3 Spoon filling into a piping bag fitted with a star-shaped nozzle and pipe filling into the chocolate shells.

Makes 32

Note: Eggs can be moulded and filled several hours in advance. Store in a covered container in a cool, dry place.

Melted Chocolate Pecan Brownies

200g dark cooking chocolate

100g butter

1½ cups white sugar

4 eggs

1 cup plain flour

½ teaspoon baking powder

1 teaspoon vanilla essence

½ cup chopped pecan nuts

1 Preheat oven to 190°C. Melt chocolate and butter together in a saucepan over a medium heat.

2 Remove from heat, stir in sugar and cool slightly. Add eggs and beat with a wooden spoon to combine. Mix in flour, baking powder and vanilla essence until smooth. Mix in pecan nuts.

3 Pour into a 20cm square cake tin lined with baking paper.

4 Bake for 30–35 minutes or until brownie mixture is set. Cut into squares.

Make 10–12

Mocha-Truffle Biscuits

(see photograph opposite)

125g butter, chopped

90g bittersweet chocolate, broken into pieces

2 tablespoons instant espresso coffee powder

2½ cups plain flour

½ cup cocoa powder

1 teaspoon baking powder

2 eggs, lightly beaten

1 cup sugar

1 cup brown sugar

2 teaspoons vanilla essence

125g pecans, chopped

1 Preheat oven to 180°C. Place the butter, chocolate and coffee powder in a heatproof bowl. Set over a saucepan of simmering water and heat, stirring, until the mixture is smooth. Remove the bowl from the pan and set aside to cool slightly.

2 Sift together the flour, cocoa powder and baking powder into a bowl. Add the eggs, sugar, brown sugar, vanilla and chocolate mixture and mix well to combine. Stir in the pecans.

3 Drop tablespoons of the mixture onto greased baking trays and bake for 12 minutes or until puffed. Stand the biscuits on trays for 2 minutes before transferring to wire racks to cool.

Makes 40

Note: This cookie version of the traditional rich truffle confection tastes delicious as an after-dinner treat with coffee.

Choc Layer Biscuits

(see photograph opposite)

125g butter

1 cup brown sugar

¾ cup sugar

2 teaspoons vanilla essence

1 egg

2¾ cups plain flour

1 teaspoon baking powder

½ cup cocoa powder

½ cup malted milk powder

1 Place the butter, brown sugar, sugar and vanilla in a bowl and beat until light and fluffy. Add the egg and beat well. Sift together the flour and the baking powder. Add the flour mixture to the butter mixture and mix to make a soft dough.

2 Divide the dough into 2 equal portions. Knead the cocoa powder into 1 portion and the malted milk powder into the other.

3 Roll out each portion of dough separately on nonstick baking paper to make a 20 x 30 cm rectangle. Place the chocolate dough on top of the malt dough and press together.

4 Cut in half lengthwise and place 1 half of dough on top of the other. You should now have 4 layers of dough in alternating colours. Place the layered dough on a tray, cover with plastic food wrap and chill for 1 hour.

5 Preheat oven to 180°C. Cut the dough into 1 cm wide fingers and place on greased baking trays. Bake for 15 minutes or until the biscuits are golden and crisp. Transfer to wire racks to cool.

Makes 40

Note: For a special occasion, dip the ends of cooled biscuits into melted white or dark chocolate and place on a wire rack until chocolate sets.

Chocolate Melting Moments

(see photograph opposite)

200g butter

2 teaspoons vanilla essence

½ cup icing sugar

1½ cups plain flour

3 tablespoons cocoa

¼ cup cornflour

CHOCOLATE CREAM

50g soft butter

1 tablespoon cocoa

½ teaspoon vanilla essence

1 teaspoon instant coffee powder

¾ cup icing sugar

1 Melt butter in a saucepan large enough to mix all the ingredients. Add vanilla essence. Sift in icing sugar, flour, cocoa and cornflour. Beat with a wooden spoon to combine.

2 Measure tablespoonfuls of mixture onto a greased oven tray. Flatten with a fork. Bake at 180°C for 15–20 minutes or until just starting to colour.

3 Cool on a wire rack. Sandwich together with chocolate cream.

CHOCOLATE CREAM

1 Place butter in a bowl. Beat in cocoa, vanilla essence, coffee powder and icing sugar until smooth.

Makes 13 pairs

Chocolate Date and Ginger Surprises

(see photograph opposite)

125g butter

½ cup sugar

1 tablespoon golden syrup

1 teaspoon vanilla essence

1¼ cups plain flour

2 tablespoons cocoa

1 teaspoon baking powder

10 pieces crystallised ginger

20 pitted dates

1 Melt butter in a saucepan large enough to mix all the ingredients. Mix in sugar and golden syrup. Remove from heat and add vanilla essence.

2 Sift flour, cocoa and baking powder into saucepan and mix to combine.

3 Cut ginger in half. Place a piece of ginger inside each date cavity. Take tablespoonfuls of dough and wrap around a ginger-stuffed date.

4 Place on a greased oven tray. Bake at 180°C for 20 minutes or until lightly golden and cooked. Cool on a wire rack.

Makes 20

Spicy Chocolate Raspberry Slice

2 cups plain flour

1 teaspoon ground cinnamon

2 tablespoons cocoa

¼ cup icing sugar

250g butter

1 cup raspberry jam

1 Sift flour, cinnamon, cocoa and icing sugar into a bowl. Melt butter and mix through dry ingredients.

2 Cut one-third off the dough and set aside. Press remaining two-thirds of dough into a 20cm square shallow tin with a baking-paper-lined base.

3 Spread with jam. Break reserved dough into small pieces and scatter over jam.

4 Bake at 180°C for 35–40 minutes or until cooked. Cut into squares or fingers while warm. Serve with fresh cream.

Makes 10–12

Sticky Fruit and Chocolate Chip Slice

(see photograph above, left)

100g butter

¼ cup honey

½ cup finely chopped dates

½ cup raisins

1 cup rice krispies

½ cup chocolate chips

1 cup dessicated coconut

1 Melt butter and honey in a saucepan large enough to mix all the ingredients. Remove from heat and mix in dates, raisins, rice krispies, chocolate chips and coconut. Mix until combined.

2 Press mixture into an 18 x 21cm shallow tin lined with a piece of baking paper to cover the base and run over two sides. Refrigerate until firm. Cut into fingers. Store in refrigerator.

Makes 10–12

Chocolate Apple Spice Slice

(see photograph above, right)

150g butter

¾ cup sugar

3 eggs

2½ cups plain flour

¼ cup cocoa

3 teaspoons baking powder

600g can spiced apple slices

icing sugar

1 Melt butter in a saucepan large enough to mix all the ingredients. Remove from heat and mix in sugar and eggs until combined. Sift in flour, cocoa and baking powder and beat with a wooden spoon until smooth.

2 Spread half the mixture into a 20 x 30cm sponge roll tin with a baking-paper-lined base. Arrange apple slices over mixture. Break up remaining dough into small pieces and scatter over apple.

3 Bake at 180°C for 30–35 minutes or until cooked. Cut into squares or fingers when cold. Dust with icing sugar.

Makes 10–12

Chocolate Orange and Pistachio Biscotti

(see photograph opposite, back)

2½ cups plain flour

1 teaspoon baking powder

¼ cup cocoa

1 cup sugar

4 eggs

2 teaspoons grated orange zest

1 cup shelled, roughly chopped
pistachio nuts

1. Sift flour, baking powder and cocoa into a bowl. Mix in sugar. Make a well in the centre of the dry ingredients. Lightly beat eggs and orange rind together. Pour into dry ingredients. Add pistachio nuts and mix until combined. Form dough into three 3cm-diameter cylinders.

2. Place on a greased and floured oven tray. Bake at 200°C for 15 minutes. Cool, then cut 1cm-wide slices on an angle from each cylinder. Place on an oven tray and bake at 200°C for a further 20 minutes.

Makes 30

Sophie's Surprises

(see photograph opposite, front)

250g butter

½ cup sugar

1 teaspoon vanilla essence

1 cup chopped pecans

1 tablespoon instant coffee powder

¼ cup cocoa

1¾ cups plain flour

1 tablespoon icing sugar

1. Melt butter in a saucepan large enough to mix all the ingredients. Remove from heat and mix in sugar, vanilla essence and pecans. Sift instant coffee, cocoa and flour into saucepan and mix until combined. Refrigerate until firm.

2. Take tablespoonfuls of mixture and roll into balls. Place on a greased oven tray and bake at 190°C for 12–15 minutes or until firm. Cool for 5 minutes then toss lightly in icing sugar.

Makes 34

Note: Use any combination of nuts depending on your preference.

Chocolate Pinwheels

125g butter

140g caster sugar

1 teaspoon vanilla essence

1 egg

220g plain flour, sifted

2 tablespoons cocoa powder, sifted

1 Preheat oven to 180°C. Place butter, sugar and vanilla essence in a mixing bowl and beat until mixture is creamy. Add egg and beat until well combined.

2 Divide mixture into two equal portions. Mix 125g flour into one portion and remaining flour and cocoa powder into the other portion.

3 Roll out each portion between two sheets of greaseproof paper to form a 20 x 30cm rectangle. Remove top sheet of paper from each and place one layer onto the other. Roll up from longer edge to form a long roll. Wrap in plastic food wrap and refrigerate for 1 hour.

4 Cut roll into 5mm slices and place on greased baking trays. Bake for 10–12 minutes or until lightly browned. Cool on wire racks.

Makes 30

Note: These are ideal last-minute biscuits. The dough can be made in advance and kept in the refrigerator until needed. Layers of plain and chocolate dough are rolled together to make these delicious and attractive biscuits.

Giant Chocolate Chip Peanut Biscuits

(see photograph opposite, front left)

200g butter

¾ cup brown sugar

½ cup sugar

1 cup smooth salt-free peanut butter

1 egg

2½ cups plain flour

½ cup cocoa

1 teaspoon baking powder

1¼ cups chocolate chips

1   Melt butter in a saucepan large enough to mix all the ingredients. Add sugars, peanut butter and egg. Stir to combine. Sift flour, cocoa and baking powder over. Add chocolate chips and mix to combine.

2   Chill mixture for 30 minutes. Measure out quarter-cupfuls of mixture and roll into balls.

3   Place on a greased baking tray and flatten with a fork. Bake at 180°C for 20 minutes or until golden.

Makes 16

Chocolate Cornflake Biscuits

(see photograph opposite, front right)

150g butter

½ cup sugar

1 egg

1 teaspoon vanilla essence

1¼ cups plain flour

1 teaspoon baking powder

½ cup cocoa

½ cup chocolate raisins

2 cups cornflakes

1   Melt butter in a saucepan large enough to mix all the ingredients. Stir in sugar. Cool. Stir in egg and vanilla essence. Sift flour, baking powder and cocoa over. Stir into butter mixture with chocolate raisins and cornflakes. Combine well.

2   Break off tablespoonfuls of dough and place on greased oven trays. Press top of biscuits with a fork. Bake at 180°C for 10–15 minutes.

Makes 25

Chocy Crisps

(see photograph opposite, back left)

150g butter

¼ cup golden syrup

1 cup sugar

1 egg

1¾ cups plain flour

2 teaspoons baking powder

2 tablespoons cocoa

1 teaspoon mixed spice

extra sugar

1   Melt butter and golden syrup in a saucepan large enough to mix all the ingredients. Remove from heat and stir in sugar. Add egg and mix well with a wooden spoon. Sift flour, baking powder, cocoa and mixed spice into saucepan and mix until combined.

2   Roll tablespoonfuls of mixture into balls and roll in extra sugar. Place on greased oven tray and flatten with a fork.

3   Bake at 180°C for 12 minutes or until golden. Leave on tray for a few minutes before moving to a wire rack to cool.

Makes 34

Double Chocolate Chip Biscuits

200g butter

3 tablespoons cocoa powder

2 teaspoons vanilla essence

½ cup pure icing sugar

1¼ cups plain flour

¼ cup cornflour

1 cup chocolate chips

1 Preheat oven to 180°C. Melt butter with cocoa in a saucepan large enough to mix all the ingredients. Remove from heat and add vanilla essence.

2 Sift together icing sugar, flour and cornflour. Mix with cocoa mixture until partly combined then add chocolate chips and mix until thoroughly combined.

3 Take about two tablespoons of mixture at a time, roll into balls and place on a greased oven tray. Flatten with the back of a spoon.

4 Bake for 15–20 minutes or until biscuits are just starting to colour. Cool on the tray until firm then remove to a wire rack.

Makes 18

Note: Macadamia nuts are often used in combination with chocolate chips. Try them in these biscuits or add chopped walnuts or pecans. If you want to make a biscuit without the chocolate chips but with other goodies, use this as a basic recipe, omitting the chocolate chips and substituting ingredients of your choice.

Rich Double-Chocolate Whoppers

(see photograph opposite, back)

250g butter

1¼ cups chocolate chips

1 cup brown sugar

1 egg

2 teaspoons vanilla essence

3 cups plain flour

2 teaspoons baking powder

1 Melt butter in a saucepan large enough to mix all the ingredients. Remove from heat and add half the chocolate bits. Stir until melted. Mix in sugar, egg and vanilla essence, beating with a wooden spoon until combined. Sift in flour and baking powder. Add remaining chocolate chips. Mix until combined.

2 Roll mixture into an 8cm-diameter cylinder. Wrap in plastic warp and refrigerate until firm.

3 Cut into 1cm slices and place on a greased oven tray. Bake at 180°C for 15–20 minutes or until biscuits are lightly golden and cooked.

Makes 30

Afghans

(see photograph opposite, front right)

175g butter

½ cup sugar

3 tablespoons cocoa

1¼ cups plain flour

2 cups cornflakes

chocolate icing

walnut halves

1 Place butter, sugar and cocoa in a saucepan large enough to mix all the ingredients. Heat until butter melts. Remove from heat. Mix in flour and cornflakes. Spoon mounds of mixture onto a greased oven tray, pressing together with the fingertips if necessary.

2 Bake at 180°C for 15 minutes or until set. When cold, ice with chocolate icing and decorate each biscuit with a walnut half.

Makes 16

Apricot and White Chocolate Biscuits

(see photograph opposite, front left)

250g butter

½ cup golden syrup

1 cup chopped dried apricots

1 teaspoon bicarbonate of soda

¼ cup hot milk

1 cup plain flour

1 cup sugar

2 cups dessicated coconut

2 cups rolled oats

1 cup white chocolate bits

1 Place butter, golden syrup and apricots in a saucepan large enough to mix all the ingredients. Heat until butter has melted. Cool. Dissolve bicarbonate of soda in milk. Add flour, sugar, coconut, rolled oats, white chocolate bits and milk mixture to saucepan. Mix to combine.

2 Drop tablespoonfuls of mixture onto a lightly greased oven tray. Bake at 180°C for 15–17 minutes or until golden.

Makes 50

Chocolate Tuilles

(see photograph opposite, back left)

75g butter

2 egg whites

½ cup caster sugar

5 tablespoons plain flour

1 tablespoon cocoa

½ teaspoon vanilla essence

1 Melt butter. Cool. Beat egg whites and sugar together until combined but not frothy. Sift flour and cocoa into egg whites. Fold in with butter and vanilla essence until combined.

2 Place teaspoonfuls of mixture on a greased oven tray, allowing room for spreading. Bake at 190°C for 8–10 minutes or until edges of tuilles start to turn golden. Leave biscuits on the tray for about 30 seconds to firm a little, then carefully lift each biscuit and place over a rolling pin. When firm, place on a wire rack until cold.

Makes 26

Note: Store these in an airtight container and use them to serve with coffee or as part of a dessert platter.

Chocolate Fingers

(see photograph opposite, back right)

2 cups plain flour

¾ cup sugar

1½ teaspoons baking powder

3 tablespoons cocoa

175g butter

1 egg

1 teaspoon vanilla essence

150g white chocolate melts

1 Place flour, sugar, baking powder and cocoa in a bowl. Mix to combine. Melt butter. Lightly beat egg and vanilla essence. Add butter and the egg mixture to bowl. Mix to combine. Measure tablespoonfuls of mixture and form into 5cm-long cylinders.

2 Place on a greased oven tray. Bake at 180°C for 15 minutes or until cooked. Cool on a wire rack. Melt chocolate to packet directions. Dip both ends of each biscuit and place over a rolling pin. When firm, place on a wire rack until cold.

Makes 36

Chocolate Loves

(see photograph opposite, front)

2 sheets sweet shortcrust pastry

¼ cup chocolate hazelnut spread

1 egg white

2 tablespoons sugar

½ cup sliced almonds

50g chocolate melts

1 Place pastry sheets on a lightly floured board. Spread with chocolate hazelnut spread. Cut heart shapes out of pastry using a 9cm heart-shaped cutter. Lightly beat egg white to break it up but don't make it frothy. Mix in sugar.

2 Place pastry hearts on a lightly floured oven tray. Brush with egg white mixture and sprinkle with almonds. Bake at 190°C for 10 minutes or until lightly golden. Cool on a wire rack. Melt chocolate to packet directions. When hearts are cold, drizzle with melted chocolate.

Makes 12

Chocolate Orange and Walnut Slice

150g butter

1 tablespoon golden syrup

½ cup brown sugar

2 teaspoons grated orange zest

½ cup chopped walnuts

1 cup crushed Weetabix crumbs or
  4 crushed Weetabix

1 cup plain flour

1 teaspoon baking powder

2 tablespoons cocoa

CHOCOLATE ORANGE ICING

¼ cup sweetened condensed milk

1 cup icing sugar

1 tablespoon cocoa

1 tablespoon orange juice

1 Melt butter, golden syrup and brown sugar in a saucepan large enough to mix all the ingredients. Remove from heat and mix in orange rind, walnuts and Weetabix. Sift in flour, baking powder and cocoa, and mix until well combined.

2 Press into a 20cm square, shallow tin with a baking-paper-lined base. Bake at 180°C for 20 minutes or until lightly golden.

3 Ice with chocolate orange icing while still warm. Cut into squares or fingers.

CHOCOLATE ORANGE ICING

1 Mix condensed milk, icing sugar, cocoa and orange juice together until smooth.

Makes 10–12

cakes and muffins

Chocolate Boxes

500g pound madeira or light fruit cake

SYRUP

1 cup water

½ cup sugar

1 strip lemon or orange rind

2–3 teaspoons rum or liqueur (optional)

BOXES

200g dark cooking chocolate

1¼ cups double cream, whipped

chocolate scrolls or strawberries
  to decorate

1   Even off the top of the pound cake and cut lengthwise down the centre, then crosswise into 4, making 8 cubes of cake. Place on a wire rack over a tray.

2   Simmer the syrup ingredients together for 8–10 minutes then remove the rind. Spoon the syrup over each cake cube until sufficient syrup has been absorbed.

3   Break up the chocolate and place in a bowl over simmering water; stir gently as the chocolate melts.

4   Take 2 pieces of cooking paper and mark a square 20 x 25cm on each. Divide the chocolate and spread in a thin layer using a pallet knife or spatula to cover each squares. Allow to set.

5   Trim the edges of each square and cut the 25cm length into 5 rows, 5cm wide. Cut each row into 4cm-wide pieces giving 20 pieces 4 x 5cm each from each square. You will then have a few spares in case of breakages.

6   Using a round-bladed knife, spread whipped cream onto a rough side of the chocolate square and press, high side upright, onto the side of a cake cube. Repeat with the 3 remaining sides to form a chocolate box.

7   When all 8 boxes are assembled, pipe a rosette of cream into the top recess. Garnish with a chocolate scroll and strawberry slice or with a chocolate-dipped strawberry. Serve with coffee or as a dessert on a bed of raspberry sauce (see page 85).

CHOCOLATE SCROLL SHAPES

1   Make a piping bag according to the directions on page 8. Then pipe out the chocolate to make spiral scroll shapes on a piece of baking paper. Remove when cool and use to decorate your boxes.

CHOCOLATE-DIPPED STRAWBERRIES

1   Leave strawberries on stem. Dip half the strawberry into the melted chocolate and place on a sheet of cooking paper until set.

Makes 8

Yule Log

5 eggs, separated

¼ cup caster sugar

100g dark chocolate, melted and cooled

2 tablespoons self-raising flour, sifted

2 tablespoons cocoa powder, sifted

chocolate shavings

WHITE CHOCOLATE FILLING

60g white chocolate

170ml double cream

CHOCOLATE ICING

200g dark chocolate, melted

60g butter, melted

1 Preheat oven to 180°C. Place egg yolks and sugar in a bowl and beat until thick and pale. Stir in chocolate, flour and cocoa powder.

2 Place egg whites in a clean bowl and beat until stiff peaks form. Fold egg whites into chocolate mixture.

3 Pour mixture into a greased and lined 26 x 32cm Swiss roll tin and bake for 15 minutes or until firm. Turn cake onto a tea towel sprinkled with caster sugar and roll up to make a long roll. Set aside to cool.

4 To make filling, place white chocolate in a heatproof bowl set over a saucepan of simmering water and heat, stirring, until smooth. Add cream and stir until combined. Cover and chill until thickened and of a spreadable consistency.

5 Unroll cake and spread with filling, leaving a 1cm border. Re-roll cake.

6 To make icing, combine melted chocolate and butter and mix until combined. Spread icing over roll, then use a fork to roughly texture the icing. Decorate log with chocolate shavings.

Serves 8

Note: Keep this dessert refrigerated until served. Dust log with pure icing sugar to create a look of fallen snow just before serving.

Choc-Meringue Cake

HAZELNUT MERINGUE

155g hazelnuts, ground

2 tablespoons cornflour

1¼ cups sugar

6 egg whites

CHOCOLATE FILLING

220g unsalted butter

185g dark chocolate, melted

3 tablespoons caster sugar

500ml full cream

2 tablespoons brandy

125g hazelnuts, ground

CHOCOLATE TOPPING

155g dark chocolate

2 teaspoons vegetable oil

whipped cream, for decoration

1 To make meringue, mix together ground hazelnuts, cornflour and ¾ cup sugar. Beat egg whites until soft peaks form, add remaining sugar a little at a time and beat until thick and glossy. Fold into hazelnut mixture.

2 Mark three 20cm squares on baking paper and place paper on baking trays. Place meringue mixture in a piping bag fitted with a small plain nozzle and pipe mixture to outline squares, then fill squares with piped lines of mixture. Bake at 120°C for 40–50 minutes, or until crisp and dry.

3 To make filling, beat butter until soft. Add chocolate, caster sugar and cream and beat until thick. Fold in brandy and hazelnuts.

4 To make topping, place chocolate and oil in the top of a double saucepan and heat over simmering water, stirring until chocolate melts and mixture is smooth. Remove top pan and set aside to cool.

5 To assemble cake, place a layer of meringue on a serving plate and spread with half the filling. Top with another meringue layer and remaining filling. Cut remaining meringue into squares and position at angles on top of cake. Drizzle with topping and decorate with cream.

Serves 10

Austrian Maple Spice Cake

CAKE

3 cups plain flour

3 teaspoons baking powder

2 tablespoons cinnamon

1 teaspoon ground cloves

2 teaspoons ground ginger

2 tablespoons Dutch cocoa powder

1 cup pure maple syrup

½ cup of honey

1½ cups caster sugar

1½ cups of buttermilk

1 teaspoon pure vanilla essence

GLAZE

200g dark cooking chocolate

2 tablespoons butter

juice and zest of 1 small orange

3 tablespoons marmalade or apricot jam

4 tablespoons sugar

2 teaspoons water

1   Butter a non-stick 28cm or 26cm springform tin and set aside. Preheat the oven to 170°C.

2   In a large bowl, mix together the flour, baking powder, cinnamon, ground cloves, ginger and cocoa. In a separate bowl, whisk the maple syrup, honey, sugar, buttermilk and vanilla. Gently but thoroughly combine the flour mixture and the syrup mixture.

3   Pour the batter into the prepared cake tin and bake for 1 hour and 10 minutes, until the cake is 'springy' when pressed gently in the centre. Remove the cake from the oven and cool thoroughly in the tin.

4   When the cake is cold, remove it from the cake tin and set aside.

5   To make the glaze, melt the chocolate and butter, either in the microwave or in a bowl resting over a saucepan of simmering water. When melted, whisk in the orange juice thoroughly.

6   Meanwhile, warm the marmalade or jam and gently spread it over the surface of the cake. Allow to cool.

7   When the chocolate mixture is smooth, carefully pour it over the marmalade-topped cake and spread it to cover.

8   Cut the zest of the orange into long fine strips (you can use a zester for this). Heat the sugar and water together in a small saucepan and, add the orange zest and simmer for 5 minutes. Lift out the caramelised orange zest and allow to cool. Discard the remaining syrup.

9   Before serving, pile the caramelised orange zest in the centre of the cake.

Serves 12

Note: This is one of the most delicious cakes you will ever eat. Moist and flavoursome, it is crowned by a rich chocolate glaze over a thin layer of marmalade. This cake follows the tradition of the 'Sacher Torte', the famous Austrian cake created by the Hotel Sacher and would make a perfect gift for your loved ones.

Vanilla Bean Tiramisu

1 vanilla bean

2 eggs, separated

½ cup caster sugar

250g cream cheese

250g mascarpone

1 cup strong black coffee, cooled

¼ cup Kahlua or Tia Maria liqueur

22 sponge finger biscuits

chocolate to garnish

1 Cut the vanilla beans in half and scrape out the seeds.

2 Combine the egg yolks, sugar and cream cheese in a mixing bowl. Beat together with electric beaters until light. Add the mascarpone and vanilla beans and stir to combine.

3 In a separate bowl, beat the egg whites together until soft peaks form. Fold the egg whites into the cream mixture.

4 Mix the coffee and liqueur together in shallow dish. Dip each biscuit in the coffee mixture.

5 Place half the biscuits in a 20cm dish. Spoon over half the cream mixture and top with the remaining biscuits and cream mixture.

6 Garnish with grated chocolate. Cover and place in the fridge for 2 hours or overnight.

Serves 6–8

Note: Savoiardi biscuits are readily available in supermarkets. Tiramisu is best made the day before. It is best to use eggs at room temperature, so remove the eggs from the fridge 3 hours before preparation.

New York Chocolate Cake

455g dark or bittersweet chocolate

455g butter

1 cup espresso or other very strong coffee

1 cup packed brown sugar

8 large eggs

900g fresh or frozen raspberries, thawed

juice of 1 lemon

2 tablespoons sugar

500g fresh raspberries

1 Preheat the oven to 180°C and butter a 24cm non-stick cake tin or long non-stick loaf tin (not springform). Chop the chocolate and place in a large heatproof bowl.

2 In a small saucepan, bring the butter, espresso and sugar to the boil and simmer briefly. Pour the liquid over the chopped chocolate and allow to sit for a few minutes. Stir the ingredients gently to help the chocolate melt. Beat the eggs, then add to the chocolate mixture, whisking thoroughly.

3 Pour the batter into the prepared cake tin, then place the tin in a large roasting pan or baking dish. Pour in hot (not boiling) water into the roasting pan to reach halfway up the sides of the cake tin, then bake for 1 hour. Remove the cake from the water bath and chill overnight.

4 The next day, remove the cake from the tin. If this is difficult, fill the kitchen sink with about 4 cm of boiling water and dip the cake tin base in the water for a few seconds to loosen the cake. Run a knife or spatula around the tin then invert the cake onto a platter.

5 To make the raspberry sauce, purée the thawed berries and their juice with the lemon juice and sugar. Pour the sauce through a sieve then chill for up to 2 days. Although it will not taste sweet, the acidity will be a perfect foil for the cake. Serve the cake with raspberry sauce and fresh raspberries. You may like to serve a little fresh cream on the side.

Serves 12

Mexican Chocolate Cake

CAKE

2 cups plain flour

2 teaspoons baking powder

1 cup of Dutch cocoa powder

1 tablespoon cinnamon

370g butter, softened

2½ cups sugar

2 teaspoons vanilla essence

6 large eggs

3 tablespoons instant coffee powder

3 tablespoons hot water

1 cup buttermilk

GANACHE

½ cup full cream

½ teaspoon cinnamon

1 tablespoon instant coffee powder

200g milk chocolate, grated

GLAZE

145g bittersweet chocolate, chopped

2 tablespoons butter

2 tablespoons corn or golden syrup

1 Preheat the oven to 180°C and butter a 28cm non-stick springform cake tin, lining the base with baking paper. Mix together the flour, baking powder, cocoa and cinnamon and set aside.

2 Cream the butter and sugar together with the vanilla and beat until the mixture is thick and light. Add the eggs, 1 at a time, beating well after each addition.

3 In a jug, mix together the coffee powder with the hot water then add the buttermilk.

4 Using a wooden spoon or spatula, mix half the flour and buttermilk mixture into the creamed egg/sugar mixture and combine gently. Add the remaining flour and buttermilk mixtures and combine thoroughly.

5 Pour the batter into the prepared cake tin and bake for 55 minutes, until firm on top and 'springy' when you gently press the surface. Allow to cool then remove from the tin.

6 To make the ganache, simmer together the cream, cinnamon and coffee powder, then pour this hot mixture over the grated chocolate. Allow to sit for a few minutes then stir gently to combine. Allow to cool. When cool, spread the ganache over the top of the cake then chill.

7 For the glaze, place the chopped chocolate, butter and syrup in a bowl over simmering water and mix until smooth. Allow to cool a little, then gently drizzle over the ganache, covering it entirely. Chill the cake, then allow to come to room temperature before serving.

Serves 10

Note: Traditional Mexican cooks have used chocolate for centuries. They mix bitter chocolate with their chilli and mole sauces to add body and richness. Here the Mexican love of chocolate is adapted to a rich, decadent dessert, topped with a milk chocolate ganache. Save this one for special occasions.

Chocolate Cheesecake

BASE

200g low-fat digestive biscuits

100g unsalted butter, at room temperature

1 tablespoon white sugar

¼ teaspoon ground cinnamon (optional)

FILLING

400g full-fat cream cheese, at room temperature

2 eggs

145g caster sugar

200g bittersweet chocolate, broken into pieces

⅔ cup sour cream

1 tablespoon dark rum (optional)

125g strawberries, halved, to decorate (optional)

1 To make the base, place the biscuits into a plastic bag then crush with a rolling pin to make crumbs. Place in a large bowl, then mix in the butter and sugar. Add the cinnamon, if using, and mix again. Press the mixture evenly into the base and up the sides of a 23cm loose-bottomed flan tin. Refrigerate until needed.

2 Preheat the oven to 180°C. In a large bowl, beat the cheese with a wooden spoon until soft and fluffy. Lightly beat the eggs in a small bowl, then gradually beat them into the cheese with the sugar. Stir until the mixture is smooth. Set aside.

3 Melt the chocolate in a small bowl set over a saucepan of simmering water, stirring frequently. Remove from the heat and stir in the sour cream and the rum, if using. Mix well.

4 Stir the chocolate mixture into the cheese mixture, then pour over the cookie base. Bake for 30 minutes or until the edges of the mixture look set (the middle may still look moist). Turn the heat off and leave the cheesecake to cool for 1 hour in the oven, with the door open.

5 Place the cheesecake in the fridge for 2 hours. If using strawberries, arrange them around the edge of the cheesecake before serving.

Serves 8

Raspberry and White Chocolate-Filled Warm Mini Chocolate Muffins

CAKE

220g butter

1 teaspoon instant coffee granules

¾ cup hot water

100g dark cooking chocolate

½ cup caster sugar

1½ cups plain flour

1½ teaspoons baking powder

2 tablespoons cocoa powder

1 egg

2 teaspoons vanilla essence

90g white chocolate, chopped finely

125g raspberries

SAUCE

1 cup pure cream

1 cup fine dark chocolate, chopped

2 tablespoons Kahlua coffee liqueur

1 Preheat the oven to 150°C. In a small saucepan, melt the butter, coffee granules and hot water together until smooth then remove from the heat.

2 Add the cooking chocolate and sugar, and stir thoroughly until the chocolate has dissolved. Sift together the flour, baking powder and cocoa, then add to the liquid chocolate mixture and mix well. Whisk the eggs and vanilla, then add to the chocolate mixture.

3 Prepare 10–12 muffin cups (or 2 trays of 6 cups each) by lightly greasing them, then dusting lightly with flour. Tip out excess flour. Place 2 tablespoons of batter into each of the muffin cups, then add a spoonful of white chocolate and some raspberries to the centre of each muffin cup. Divide the remaining chocolate batter between the muffin cups and tap gently to settle the mixture.

4 Bake for 20 minutes or until firm on top when touched. When baked, remove the cakes from the oven and allow to cool in the tin for 5 minutes. Then carefully loosen each cake from the tin. Turn the muffin tray upside down on a flat tray to remove the muffins.

5 Meanwhile, make the sauce. Heat the cream until boiling, then pour it over the chocolate pieces placed in a heatproof bowl. Allow the cream and chocolate to sit for 10 minutes, then gently but thoroughly, stir the mixture. Add the coffee liqueur and stir again until smooth.

6 To serve, drizzle the chocolate sauce over the plate, then carefully place each cake in the centre of the plates. Serve with some thick cream (or vanilla-bean ice cream).

Makes 10–12

Note: If raspberries are not in season, use chopped dried apricots or fresh orange segments (well-drained) and substitute Grand Marnier or Cointreau for the coffee liqueur.

Muddy Mud Cake

225g butter

225g bittersweet chocolate, chopped

100g caster sugar

85g brown sugar

30ml brandy

1½ cups hot water

200g plain flour

1 teaspoon baking powder

3 tablespoons Dutch cocoa powder

2 eggs

1 teaspoon vanilla essence

icing sugar, for dusting

cream or ice cream, for serving

1 Preheat the oven to 150°C and grease a 24cm non-stick, springform cake tin, or small moulds.

2 In a saucepan, melt the butter, then add the chocolate, sugars, brandy and hot water. Mix well with a whisk until the mixture is smooth.

3 Sift together the flour, baking powder and cocoa and add to the chocolate mixture with the eggs and vanilla. Beat just until combined. (Don't worry if the mixture is lumpy.)

4 Pour into the cake tin and bake in oven for 50 minutes, or if using moulds bake for 30 minutes. Allow to cool in the tin or moulds for 15 minutes, then turn out.

5 Dust with icing sugar and serve warm with cream or ice cream.

Serves 6

Chocolate-Pecan Gâteau

4 eggs, separated

¾ cup caster sugar

2 tablespoons brandy

200g pecans, roughly chopped

2 tablespoons plain flour

CHOCOLATE-BRANDY GLAZE

315g milk chocolate

2 teaspoon instant coffee powder

90ml double cream

1 tablespoon brandy

155g pecans, roughly chopped

1 Preheat the oven to 160°C. Place egg yolks, sugar and brandy in a bowl and beat until thick and pale. Place egg whites in a clean bowl and beat until stiff peaks form. Fold egg whites, pecans and flour into egg yolk mixture.

2 Pour mixture into a lightly greased and lined 23cm springform tin and bake for 40 minutes or until cake is firm. Cool in tin.

3 To make glaze, place chocolate, coffee powder, cream and brandy in a heatproof bowl set over a saucepan of simmering water and heat, stirring, until mixture is smooth. Remove bowl from pan and set aside to cool slightly. Spread glaze over top and sides of cooled cake.

4 Sprinkle pecans over top of cake and press into side of cake. Allow to set before serving.

Serves 8

Rich Dark Chocolate Cake

400g unsalted butter, plus extra
  for greasing

500g milk chocolate, broken into pieces

3 tablespoons water

350g caster sugar

6 tablespoons plain flour

6 large eggs, separated

pinch of salt

COATING

6 tablespoons seedless raspberry or
  cherry jam

200g milk chocolate, broken into pieces

3 tablespoons water

4 tablespoons single cream

2 tablespoons pure icing sugar

raspberries and fresh mint to
  decorate (optional)

1 Preheat the oven to 200°C. Grease 900g loaf tins. Melt the chocolate with water, butter and sugar in a bowl set over a saucepan of simmering water. Sift in the flour and stir, then beat in the egg yolks.

2 Place the egg whites into a bowl with a pinch of salt. Whisk until the mixture forms stiff peaks (this is easiest with an electric whisk). Fold 1 tablespoon of the whites into the chocolate mixture to loosen it, then fold in the remaining whites.

3 Divide the mixture between the tins and tap on the work surface to settle the contents. Bake for 45 minutes or until firm. Cool for 15 minutes in the tins. Turn out onto a cooling rack and leave for 2 hours or until cooled completely.

4 For the coating, heat the jam with 3 tablespoons of water in a pan until dissolved. Brush over the tops and sides of the cakes. Melt the chocolate with 3 tablespoons of water in a bowl set over a pan of simmering water, then stir in the cream and sugar. Smooth over the top and sides of the cakes, then place in the fridge for 1 hour. Decorate with raspberries and mint and dust with confectioner's sugar.

Serves 20

Chocolate Pikelets

(see photograph opposite, back left)

1 cup plain flour

¼ cup icing sugar

1 tablespoon cocoa

1 teaspoon baking powder

2 tablespoons butter

1 egg

½ cup milk

1 Sift flour, icing sugar, cocoa and baking powder into a bowl. Make a well in the centre of the dry ingredients. Melt butter. Lightly beat egg. Mix butter, egg and milk into dry ingredients until combined.

2 Cook 2 tablespoonful lots of mixture in a lightly greased frying pan. As bubbles start to appear, turn to cook the second side. Serve warm with jam, chocolate spread or butter.

Makes 12

Note: These are a great goodie to rustle up for an after-school treat.

Chocolate Hazelnut Pinwheel Scones

(see photograph opposite, back right)

2 cups plain flour

5 teaspoons baking powder

2 tablespoons sugar

50g butter

¾ cup milk

½ cup chocolate hazelnut spread

½ cup chopped roasted hazelnuts

1 Sift flour and baking powder into a bowl. Mix in sugar. Melt butter and mix through dry ingredients. Mix in enough milk to make a stiff dough.

2 Roll or pat dough out on a lightly floured board to a rectangle measuring 40 x 12cm. Spread with chocolate hazelnut spread and sprinkle nuts over.

3 Roll up from the long side like a Swiss roll. Cut into 2cm slices. Place cut-side down on a lightly floured oven tray. Bake at 220°C for 10–15 minutes or until scones are lightly golden and cooked.

Makes 20

Chocolate Devonshires

(see photograph opposite, front)

2 cups plain flour

5 teaspoons baking powder

¼ cup sugar

75g butter

½ cup chocolate sauce

¼ cup milk

raspberry jam

1 cup whipped cream

2 tablespoons chocolate sauce

raspberry sauce

1 Sift flour and baking powder into a bowl. Mix in sugar. Melt butter and mix through dry ingredients with first measure of chocolate sauce. Mix in enough milk to make a stiff dough.

2 Pat dough out on a lightly floured board to 3cm thickness. Cut into squares or rounds. Place on a baking tray and bake at 220°C for 10–12 minutes or until cooked. Cool in a tea towel.

3 When ready to serve, cut in half horizontally and spread with raspberry jam. Mix whipped cream and second measure of chocolate sauce together. Place a spoonful on top of jam and drizzle with a little raspberry sauce.

Makes 14

Note: Devonshire teas always had scones served with jam and clotted cream. For chocoholics here's your own jam and creamy version of this traditional favourite.

Chocolate Vanilla Cake

(see photograph opposite, back)

175g butter

¾ cup sugar

3 eggs

1¼ cups plain flour

2 teaspoons baking powder

1 tablespoon vanilla essence

2 tablespoons cocoa

100g white chocolate

CHOCOLATE ICING

2 tablespoons butter

50g cooking chocolate

¾ cup icing sugar

2 tablespoons hot water

1 Melt butter and sugar in a saucepan large enough to mix all the ingredients. Heat mixture until butter melts. Remove from heat. Cool slightly. Beat eggs and add to butter mixture. Sift flour and baking powder into mixture and mix with a wooden spoon until combined.

2 Divide mixture in half. Add vanilla essence to one half and mix in. Add cocoa to remaining half and mix in. Place alternate spoonfuls of mixture into a 20cm round cake tin with a baking-paper-lined base. Swirl mixtures together using a knife.

3 Bake at 180°C for 30–35 minutes or until cake springs back when lightly touched. Cool in tin for 10 minutes before turning onto a wire rack.

4 When cold, ice with chocolate icing. Grate white chocolate with a potato peeler and sprinkle over chocolate icing.

CHOCOLATE ICING

1 Melt butter and cooking chocolate in a saucepan over a low heat. Mix in icing sugar and water until combined.

Serves 6–8

Café Cupcakes

(see photograph opposite, front)

4 eggs

¾ cup caster sugar

1 teaspoon vanilla essence

50g butter

½ cup plain flour

1 teaspoon baking powder

½ cup cocoa

2 tablespoons instant coffee powder

6 x 4cm chocolate mint squares

icing sugar

finely grated chocolate

1 Beat eggs, sugar and vanilla essence together until thick and creamy. The mixture will hold a figure-of-eight shape when it reaches this stage.

2 Melt butter. Sift flour, baking powder, cocoa and coffee into egg mixture and fold in with butter.

3 Three-quarters fill greased muffin pans with mixture. Bake at 190°C for 12–15 minutes or until cakes spring back when lightly touched.

4 Cool in tins for 5 minutes before turning onto a wire rack. Cut a 1cm slit in the top of each cake. Cut chocolate mints in half diagonally and push cut side into slit in each cake. Dust cakes with icing sugar and decorate with grated chocolate.

Makes 12

Note: These are great for a special afternoon tea or teenage party. Use the idea for small cakes baked in mini-muffin pans for a child's birthday tea party. Serve these topped with cream if wished.

Chocolate Macaroon Cake

100g butter

½ cup sugar

3 egg yolks

1¼ cups plain flour

¼ cup cocoa

2 teaspoons baking powder

2 teaspoons vanilla essence

½ cup milk

½ cup cherry jam

TOPPING

3 egg whites

¼ cup sugar

1½ cups dessicated coconut

2 tablespoons cocoa

1 teaspoon almond essence

1 Melt butter in a saucepan large enough to mix all the ingredients. Remove from heat and stir in sugar and egg yolks. Mix to combine. Sift flour, cocoa and baking powder into saucepan. Add vanilla essence and milk. Mix to combine.

2 Spread mixture into a 20cm ring tin. Spoon jam over cake batter and spread topping over. Bake at 180°C for 45–50 minutes or until an inserted skewer comes out clean.

3 Cool in tin before turning out onto a tea towel–covered wire rack. Turn back onto another rack so topping is on top.

TOPPING

1 Beat egg whites until stiff. Gradually beat in sugar and continue beating until mixture is thick and glossy. Fold in coconut, cocoa and almond essence.

Serves 6–8

White Chocolate Surprise Muffins

(see photograph opposite, back left)

2 cups plain flour

3 teaspoons baking powder

½ cup sugar

1 cup white chocolate melts

50g butter

2 eggs

¾ cup milk

10 squares caramel-filled chocolate

1. Sift flour and baking powder into a bowl. Mix in sugar. Make a well in the centre of the dry ingredients. Melt white chocolate melts and butter together. Lightly beat eggs. Add milk. Pour egg mixture into dry ingredients. Stir briefly, add butter mixture and just combine ingredients.

2. Quarter fill greased deep muffin pans with mixture. Place a chocolate square in the centre of the mixture and top with enough mixture to cover the caramello and three-quarters fill the muffin pans.

3. Bake at 190°C for 15–20 minutes or until muffins spring back when lightly touched. Serve dusted with cocoa.

Makes 10

Chocolate Cherry Quick Bread

(see photograph opposite, back right)

1 cup glacé cherries

25g butter

½ cup sugar

1 tablespoon golden syrup

1 teaspoon bicarbonate of soda

1 cup boiling water

1½ cups plain flour

¼ cup cocoa

1½ teaspoons baking powder

2 tablespoons slivered almonds

1. Place cherries, butter, sugar, golden syrup and bicarbonate of soda in a bowl large enough to mix all the ingredients. Pour boiling water over and mix until butter melts. Sift in flour, cocoa and baking powder and mix quickly until just combined.

2. Pour into a 20cm loaf tin with a baking-paper-lined base. Sprinkle slivered almonds over.

3. Bake at 180°C for 40 minutes or until loaf springs back when lightly touched. Cool in tin for 10 minutes before turning onto a wire rack.

Serves 4

After-Christmas Chocolate Loaf

(see photograph opposite, front)

50g butter

1 cup boiling water

2 tablespoons golden syrup

½ cup brown sugar

1 teaspoon bicarbonate of soda

1 cup Christmas fruit mince

2 cups wholemeal flour

¼ cup cocoa

1. Place butter in a bowl large enough to mix all the ingredients. Pour boiling water over and mix in golden syrup, until butter melts. Add sugar, bicarbonate of soda, fruit mince, flour and cocoa. Mix until combined.

2. Pour into a 22cm loaf tin with a baking-paper-lined base. Bake at 180°C for 45 minutes or until loaf springs back when lightly touched. Leave in tin for 5 minutes before turning onto a wire rack to cool. Serve sliced with butter or jam.

Serves 4

Note: Sometimes you end up with a small amount of Christmas mincemeat left after Christmas. Here's a good way to use it up – perhaps for Easter.

Chocolate Date and Walnut Cake

2 cups plain flour

3 teaspoons baking powder

¼ cup cocoa

½ teaspoon bicarbonate of soda

2 cups sugar

250g soft butter

4 eggs

1 cup milk

DATE AND WALNUT FILLING

2 cups pitted dates

½ cup orange juice

70g walnut pieces

TOPPING

100g pouch chocolate melts

finely shredded orange rind

clementine segments

1 Sift flour, baking powder, cocoa and bicarbonate of soda into a mixer bowl. Add sugar, butter, eggs and milk and beat on low speed to combine. Increase speed and beat for 3 minutes.

2 Pour into a 23cm square cake tin with a baking-paper-lined base. Bake at 160°C for 1¼–1½ hours or until cake springs back when lightly touched.

3 Cool in tin for 10 minutes before turning onto a wire rack. When cold, cut in half horizontally, spread date and walnut filling on bottom half. Top with second half.

4 Drizzle top with melted chocolate and decorate with finely shredded orange rind and clementine segments.

DATE AND WALNUT FILLING

1 Roughly chop dates. Mix dates and orange juice together in a saucepan and simmer for 10 minutes. Cool, then puree in a food processor or blender. Add walnuts and process or blend until finely chopped and mixture is combined.

TOPPING

1 Melt chocolate to packet directions. Cut a corner from pouch and use as a piping bag to decorate cake.

Serves 6–8

index